MAHABHARATA
STORIES

Death of Abhimanyu

Subhadra Sen Gupta

Om KIDZ
An imprint of Om Books International

It was day twelve and the Kauravas and Pandavas were still at war. One by one, the legendary warriors had fallen in the Battle of Kurukshetra.

On the thirteenth day, Dronacharya came up with a new strategy. The Kauravas were going to make a battle formation in the shape of a discus called the chakravyuha. He knew that only very few warriors could break it.

When they heard of this plan, Bhima said to Nakul, "If we do not break the chakravyuha formation soon, the Pandava army will be destroyed." Nakul asked, "Do any of our warriors know the way to enter and break this battle formation?'

Yudhishthira said, "The only two who can succeed against the deadly chakravyuha are Arjuna and Krishna." However, they were so far away on the battlefield that it was not possible for them to come back in time.

At this point, a young warrior Abhimanyu stepped forward and said, "I know how to enter the chakravyuha." He was the son of Krishna's sister Subhadra and Arjuna.

"Who taught you?" Bhima asked.

Abhimanyu revealed that when he was still in his mother's womb, Krishna had explained the way to enter the chakravyuha to his sister. "I heard what my uncle Krishna said and know the way to break in and enter the chakravyuha."

So young Abhimanyu led the Pandava warriors towards the chakravyuha. The problem was that he knew how to enter the maze but he did not know how to destroy and break out of it. Yudhishthira promised to help him come out.

As Abhimanyu entered the chakravyuha, Jayadrath of the Kaurava army quickly moved his chariot to the entrance of the formation. And blocked the path of the other Pandava fighters who could not enter and fight beside Abhimanyu.

Inside the chakravyuha, Abhimanyu now fought alone against some of the best Kaurava warriors. The young boy fought bravely but, then against the rule of battle, he was overpowered by the Kauravas and died fighting.

By the time Arjuna and Lord Krishna reached the battlefield, Abhimanyu had been killed and Arjuna fought with fierce anger and destroyed the chakravyuha.

When Arjuna was weeping in grief beside his son, he was told of how the Kaurava warriors had killed Abhimanyu and how Jayadrath had blocked the entrance to the chakravyuha.

Hearing this, Arjuna took a terrible vow that shocked everyone, "They broke the laws of battle and Jayadrath has been the cause of my son's death. I will kill Jayadrath tomorrow by sunset or I will kill myself."

Next morning, the Kaurava warriors surrounded Jayadrath to protect him from Arjuna's wrath. The sun was dipping down past the horizon and Jayadrath was still alive.

Krishna looked up to the sky and prayed, "Do not set yet, Respected Surya." And Surya stayed shining in the sky as Arjuna's arrow found its mark and Jayadrath was dead.

At the end of the great Battle of Kurukshetra, the only child of the Pandavas to survive was Abhimanyu's baby son, Parikshit. One day, he would follow Yudhishthira to the throne of Indraprastha and Hastinapur.